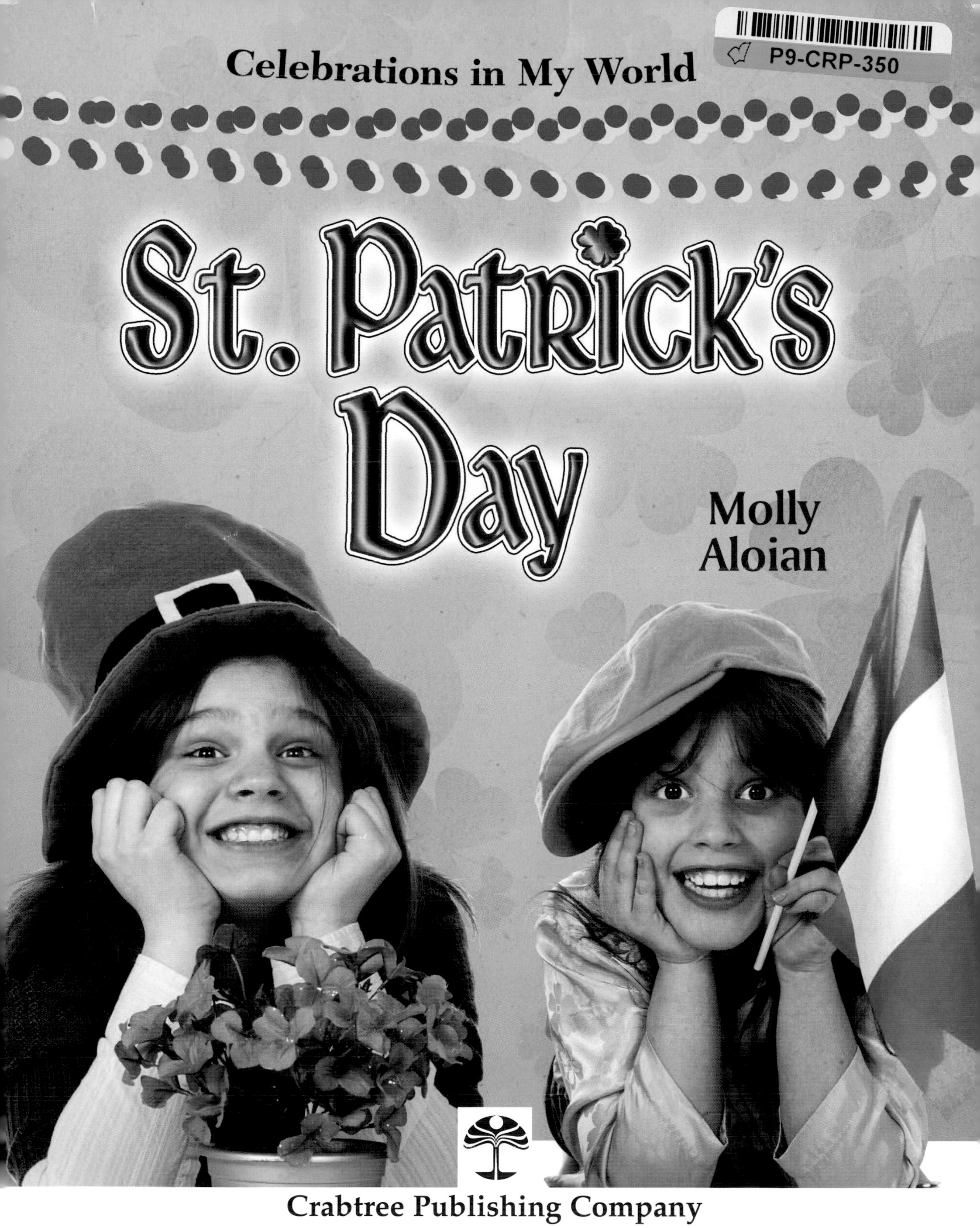

Crabtree Publishing Company
www.crabtreebooks.com

Crabtree Publishing Company
www.crabtreebooks.com

Author: Molly Aloian
Coordinating editor: Chester Fisher
Series and project editor: Penny Dowdy
Editor: Adrianna Morganelli
Proofreader: Crystal Sikkens
Editorial director: Kathy Middleton
Production coordinator: Katherine Berti
Prepress technician: Katherine Berti
Project manager: Kumar Kunal (Q2AMEDIA)
Art direction: Dibakar Acharjee (Q2AMEDIA)
Cover design: Tarang Saggar (Q2AMEDIA)
Design: Neha Kaul (Q2AMEDIA)
Photo research: Farheen Aadil (Q2AMEDIA)

Photographs:
Alamy: Adam Eastland: p. 15; Andrew Fox: p. 31; Richard Levine: p. 4
Associated Press: p. 22
Canstock Photo: Nancy Kennedy: p. 19; Phakimata: p. 10
Corbis: Bettmann: p. 12; Blaine Harrington III: p. 21; Claudia Kunin: p. 6; Ted Spiegel: p. 13
Dreamstime: Richard Gunion: p. 11; Spooky2006: p. 8
Fotolia: Jose Manuel Gelpi: p. 17; Glenda Powers: p. 1 (foreground)
Getty Images: p. 14
Jupiter Images: Bruno Barbier: p. 26
Photographers Direct: Joe Fox: p. 20; Sally Weigand: p. 16
Photolibrary: Mary Evans Picture Library: p. 5; North Wind Pictures: p. 9
Shutterstock: p. 7, 27; Gualtiero Boffi: p. 23; Sarah Bossert: p. 18; Linda Bucklin: p. 24; Mandy Godbehear: front cover; Timothy R. Nichols: p. 25; Pres Panayotov: p. 29; C Salisbury: p. 1 (background); Steve Wood: p. 28; Terrie L. Zeller: p. 30

Library and Archives Canada Cataloguing in Publication

Aloian, Molly
St. Patrick's Day / Molly Aloian.

(Celebrations in my world)
Includes index.
ISBN 978-0-7787-4758-1 (bound).--ISBN 978-0-7787-4776-5 (pbk.)

1. Saint Patrick's Day--Juvenile literature. 2. Saint Patrick's Day--History--Juvenile literature. I. Title. II. Title: Saint Patrick's Day. III. Series: Celebrations in my world

GT4995.P3A46 2010 j394.262 C2009-902028-9

Library of Congress Cataloging-in-Publication Data

Aloian, Molly.
St. Patrick's day / Molly Aloian.
p. cm. -- (Celebrations in my world)
Includes index.
ISBN 978-0-7787-4776-5 (pbk. : alk. paper) -- ISBN 978-0-7787-4758-1 (reinforced library binding : alk. paper)
1. Saint Patrick's Day--Juvenile literature. I. Title. II. Series.

GT4995.P3A46 2010
394.262--dc22

2009014153

Crabtree Publishing Company
www.crabtreebooks.com 1-800-387-7650

Printed in China/082011/FC20110523

 In Canada: We acknowledge the financial support of the Government of Canada through the Canada Book Fund for our publishing activities.

Published in Canada
Crabtree Publishing
616 Welland Ave.
St. Catharines, ON
L2M 5V6

Published in the United States
Crabtree Publishing
PMB 59051
350 Fifth Avenue, 59th Floor
New York, New York 10118

Published in the United Kingdom
Crabtree Publishing
Maritime House
Basin Road North, Hove
BN41 1WR

Published in Australia
Crabtree Publishing
386 Mt. Alexander Rd.
Ascot Vale (Melbourne)
VIC 3032

Contents

What is St. Patrick's Day?

St. Patrick's Day is a holiday. People celebrate St. Patrick's Day each year on March 17. Irish people have been celebrating this holiday for over one thousand years! People from other backgrounds like to celebrate, too.

These children are performing in a St. Patrick's Day parade in New York City.

DID YOU KNOW?

Millions of people living in the United States and Canada have Irish ***ancestors****.*

The holiday honors Saint Patrick.

On St. Patrick's Day, people **honor** and remember Saint Patrick. People use "St." as a short form for the word "Saint." Saint Patrick was a **priest** in **Ireland**. The story of Saint Patrick spread around the world.

Young Patrick

Many people believe that Patrick was born in England. His family was rich. When Patrick was just 16 years old, he was kidnapped. His kidnappers took him to Ireland. They forced him to be a slave.

Saint Patrick was forced to work as a shepherd.

DID YOU KNOW?

A shepherd is a person who takes care of sheep. A shepherd spends a lot of time alone in fields.

Patrick's life was hard, and he was lonely. He prayed and had visions. One day, he heard a voice telling him to run away. Patrick escaped on a ship. When he was finally free, he went back home and began studying religion. He became a priest.

This statue was built in honor of Saint Patrick.

Return to Ireland

In his prayers, Patrick heard God tell him to go back to Ireland. Patrick returned to the land where he was a slave. He traveled from village to village teaching people about Christianity.

Many Irish people followed druids. Druids believed in gods of nature. People thought that druids had magical powers and could see the future. The druids tried to kill Patrick but he refused to leave Ireland.

- Patrick wanted people to read the Bible.

Druids held ceremonies in forests.

DID YOU KNOW?

Ireland has no snakes. Some people believe Saint Patrick made all the snakes leave Ireland.

Becoming a Saint

In Ireland, Patrick performed miracles, helped build hundreds of churches and schools, and offered kindness to many sick people. He died on March 17 in the year 461.

Irish people loved him so much that they made him a saint. In Ireland, there are more than 60 churches named after Saint Patrick.

- Saint Patrick's Cathedral in New York was named after Saint Patrick.

DID YOU KNOW?

Many churches and schools around the world have been named after Saint Patrick.

This image of Saint Patrick is made out of stained glass.

Irish Immigrants

During the 1700s, many Irish people left Ireland and went to live in America. Many of these Irish **immigrants** lived in New York and Boston. In 1737, Boston held the first American St. Patrick's Day celebration.

Irish immigrants brought their families and traditions to America.

DID YOU KNOW?

Irish people are very proud to be Irish. The phrase "Erin Go Bragh" means "Ireland forever."

People gather today to celebrate just as they did in the 1700s.

A group of immigrants, called the Charitable Irish Society, organized the celebration. Each year, more and more people wanted to take part in the celebration and spend time with other Irish people.

Around the World

During the 1800s, a disaster called the Great Potato **Famine**, struck Ireland. People living there did not have enough food. More than one million Irish people left to go to the United States. Hundreds of thousands went to Canada. Many others went to England and Australia, as well as other countries.

People starved during the Great Potato Famine.

Irish immigrants continued to celebrate St. Patrick's Day in their new homes. In Australia, the cities of Sydney and Brisbane hold parades each year. Montreal's St. Patrick's Day parade is the oldest in Canada.

A girl in Tokyo, Japan, carries the Japanese and Irish flags in a St. Patrick's Day parade.

DID YOU KNOW?

There are three colors on the Irish flag, green, white, and orange. The flag is called the Tricolor. "Tri" means three.

Feeling Green

Green is Ireland's national color. The color green reminds people of St. Patrick's Day. Many people decorate their homes, offices, schools, and businesses with green decorations to celebrate the holiday.

People hang decorations to get ready for St. Patrick's Day.

DID YOU KNOW?

Ireland is also called the ***Emerald*** *Isle. Emeralds are green stones. Ireland is called the Emerald Isle because the country has many green fields.*

Green streamers, tablecloths, and banners are popular decorations. People wear green clothes, shoes, and hats to honor Saint Patrick and Ireland. This tradition is often called "the wearing of the green."

People show their pride by wearing green on St. Patrick's Day.

St. Patrick's Day Foods

People eat special foods to celebrate St. Patrick's Day. Some people eat Irish stew, which is made of lamb, potatoes, and other vegetables. Corned beef and cabbage are other popular St. Patrick's Day foods.

Corned beef and cabbage make a delicious St. Patrick's Day meal.

DID YOU KNOW?

On St. Patrick's Day, many people add green food coloring to their drinks!

Irish soda bread tastes best when it is still warm.

Some people also eat Irish soda bread. It is a cake-like bread that uses baking soda instead of **yeast** to make the bread rise. Some people add raisins or nuts. To celebrate St. Patrick's Day, ask an adult to help you make green Jell-O, green drinks, green cupcakes, or green pancakes.

Irish Music

Many people listen to or sing Irish songs on St. Patrick's Day. Traditional St. Patrick's Day songs include "Danny Boy," "Too-Ra-Loo-Ra-Loo-Ral," "My Wild Irish Rose," and "When Irish Eyes are Smiling."

People celebrate St. Patrick's Day by making music.

DID YOU KNOW?

Irish people have been playing fiddles and tin whistles for hundreds of years.

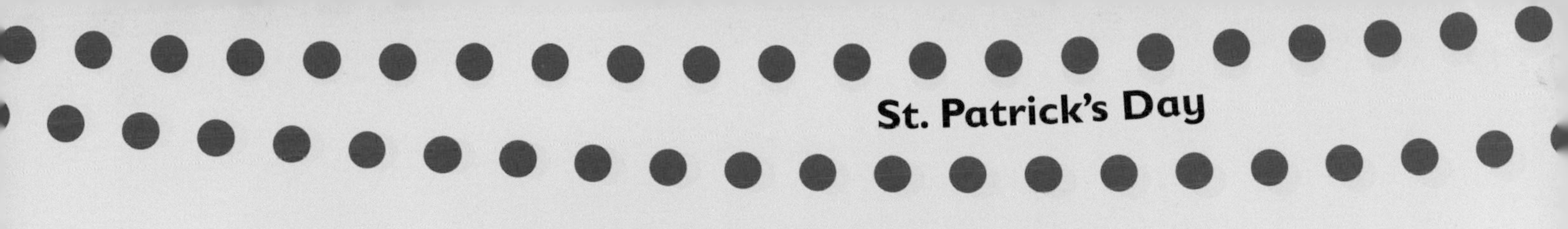

Irish dancers perform for an audience.

Certain instruments are traditional for Irish music. People play bagpipes or harps to celebrate St. Patrick's Day. The harp is one of Ireland's oldest instruments. Irish dancers perform **jigs** or **clogging** routines as people play their instruments.

Shamrocks

Do you know what a shamrock is? A shamrock is a small green plant that usually has three leaves. It is a type of clover. A shamrock is a **symbol** for Ireland. A symbol is something that stands for something else.

The Boston Celtics basketball team uses the shamrock as an emblem on their uniforms.

DID YOU KNOW?

Some people believe that it is lucky to find a four-leaf clover.

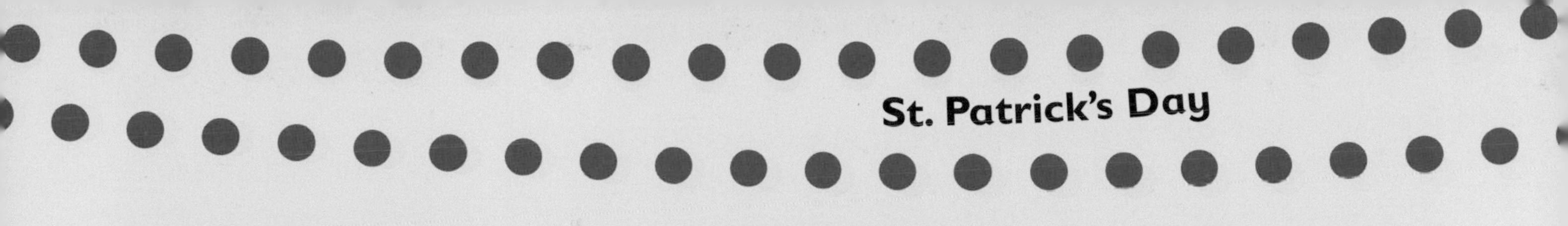

Each leaf on the shamrock represents a part in the Holy Trinity.

According to legend, Saint Patrick used the shamrock's three leaves to teach people about the Christian Holy Trinity—the Father, the Son, and the **Holy Spirit**. The word "trinity" means something that has three parts.

Leprechauns

The leprechaun is another symbol of St. Patrick's Day. A leprechaun is a magical spirit. Leprechauns are little men who dress in green and carry tools. They fix the shoes of Irish fairies who love to dance.

The fairies leave gold coins for the leprechauns to thank them for their work. The leprechauns save their gold in large pots.

- In Ireland long ago, people believed that leprechauns were mean.

DID YOU KNOW?

Some people dress up as leprechauns or fairies to celebrate St. Patrick's Day.

There are many stories about people who have searched for a leprechaun's pot of gold.

St. Patrick's Day Parades

Parades are an important part of St. Patrick's Day celebrations. People march, wave Irish flags, and cheer. Parades also have music and dancing. Children dress up and march in parades, too.

These children are waving Irish flags.

DID YOU KNOW?

Many cities in North America, including Boston, New York, Philadelphia, Chicago, and Montreal, have parades on St. Patrick's Day.

Marching in a parade honors and celebrates Irish-Americans.

One of the largest St. Patrick's Day parades is in New York City. Almost three million people watch the parade each year. New Yorkers have been marching in the St. Patrick's Day parade for more than 200 years!

Green River

In Illinois, the Chicago Journeymen Plumbers dye the Chicago River green on St. Patrick's Day. The green water lasts for just one day. It is not harmful to the animals or plants in the water.

Over 100,000 people watch the Chicago River turn green each year.

DID YOU KNOW?

The dye put in the Chicago River looks orange at first. Then it turns green.

On St. Patrick's Day the lights on the Empire State Building are changed to green.

In Sydney, Australia, green water shoots from the city fountains. In London, England, the St. Patrick's Day festival features Irish food, dance, crafts, and music. In New York, the Empire State Building shines with green lights.

Irish for a Day!

You do not have to be Irish to celebrate St. Patrick's Day. Anyone can celebrate in their own way. It is a great day to spend time with friends and family and enjoy an Irish meal together.

This child is making St. Patrick's Day decorations.

DID YOU KNOW?

People often request green flowers for St. Patrick's Day parades and celebrations.

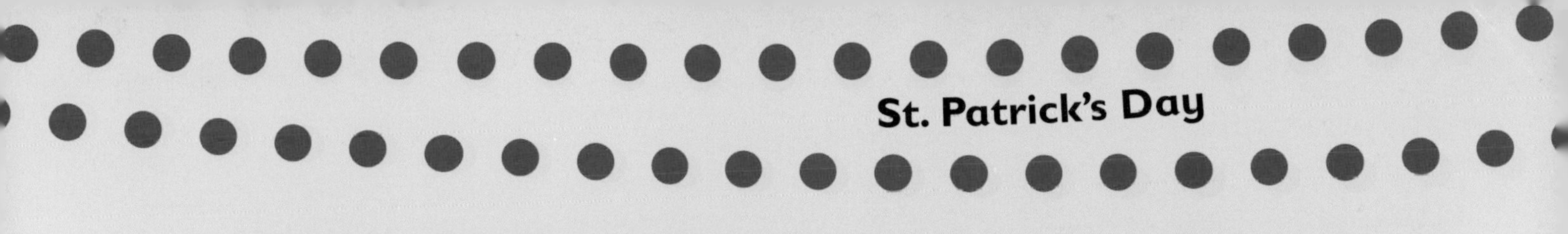

These children are having fun on St. Patrick's Day.

In Ireland, St. Patrick's Day is a religious holiday. People attend church for special services. People in the United States and Canada may also go to church. It is the perfect day to celebrate Saint Patrick and the history and traditions of Irish people.

Glossary

ancestor A person from whom an individual or group is descended

clogging A dance in which the dancers wear special shoes called clogs

emerald A green gem

famine A shortage of food

Holy Spirit The third part of the Christian Trinity

honor To respect or admire

immigrant A person who comes to a country to live

Ireland An island near Great Britain surrounded by the North Atlantic Ocean

jig A lively, bouncy dance

priest An important member of a church

symbol Something that stands for something else

yeast The substance that makes bread rise

Index